Odom Ministries
Sarah B. Odom, PhD

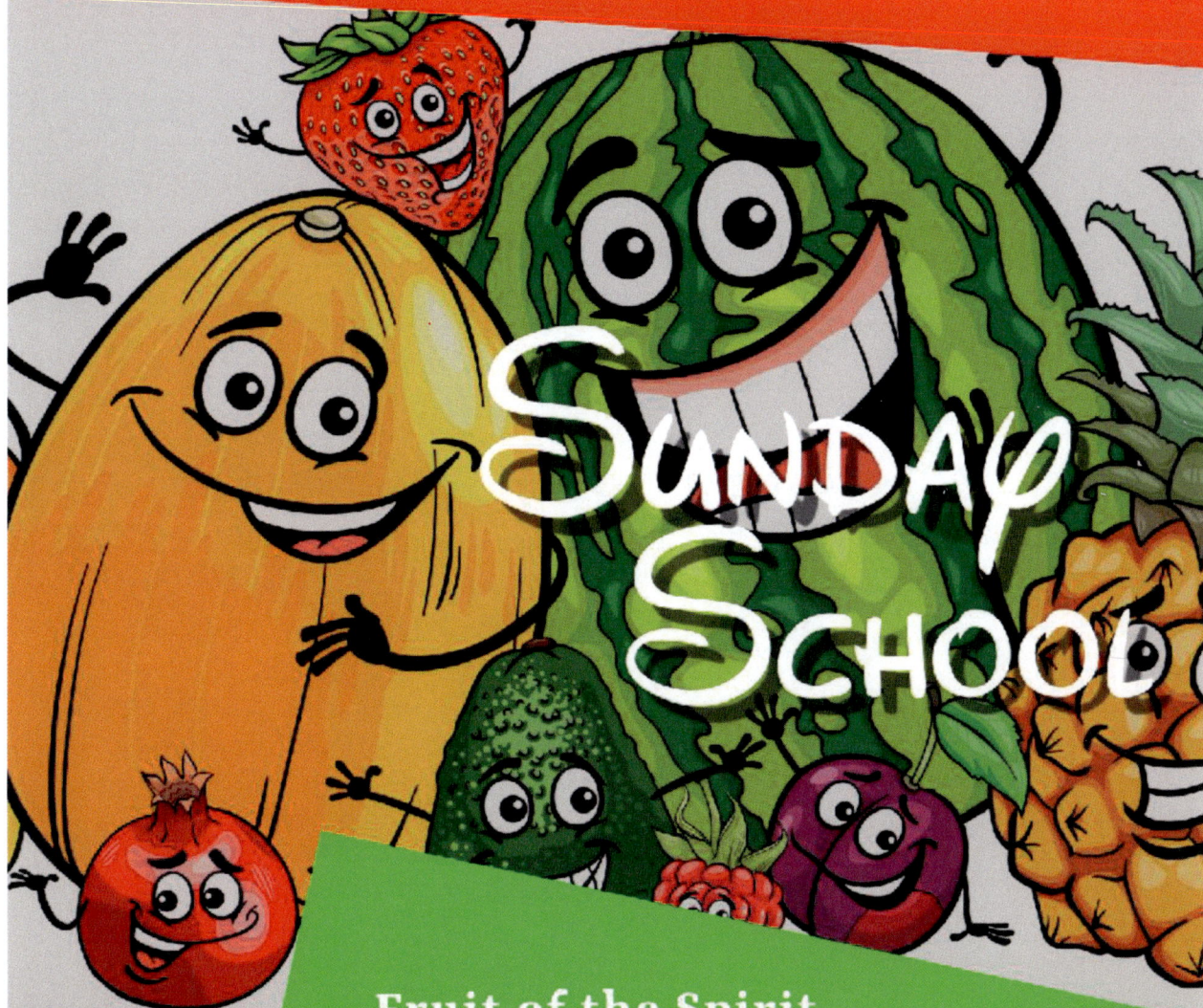

Sunday School

Fruit of the Spirit
Sunday School Lessons

Dedication

This set of lessons is dedicated to our wonderful children at the Lighthouse of Living Faith Church. I love you all dearly, and I hope you enjoy these lessons. Live every day with the Fruit of the Spirit in your life. Be sweet! Be encouraging! Be kind! Be good! Serve the Lord with all your hearts!

Love,

Mimsy

Odom Ministries
Sarah B. Odom, PhD

SUNDAY SCHOOL

Fruit of the Spirit
Sunday School Lessons

LOVE & JOY

Bearing Fruit for Jesus

Love

Here are a few Bible Verses about LOVE:

Love is patient, love is kind.

Do everything in love.

Dear friends, let us love one another, for love comes from God.

For God so loved the world that he gave his one and only Son, that whoever believes in him shall not perish but have eternal life.

Joy

Here are a few Bible Verses about JOY:

Clap your hands, all you nations; shout to God with cries of joy.

Shout aloud and sing for joy, people of Zion, for great is the Holy One of Israel among you.

For the kingdom of God is not a matter of eating and drinking, but of righteousness, peace and joy in the Holy Spirit

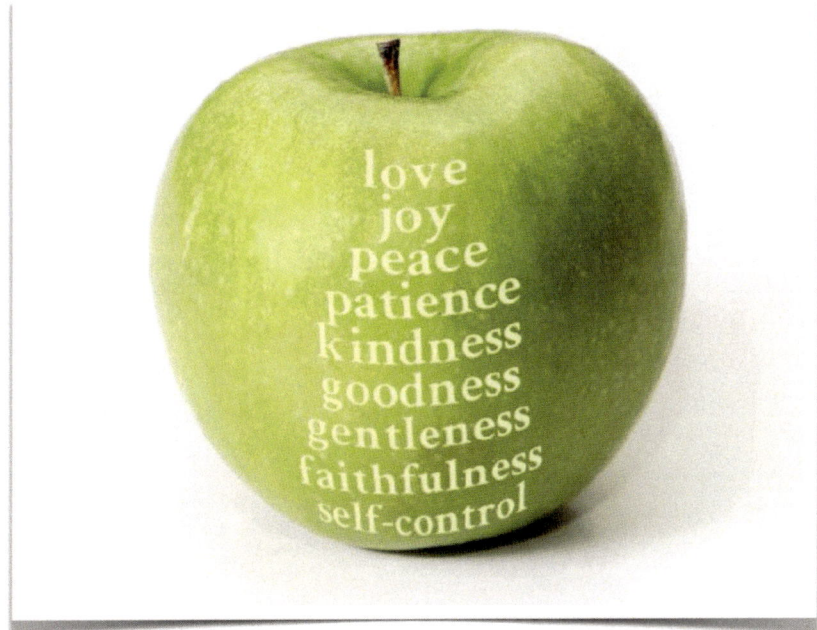

Love

The Apostle Paul was a very important man in the Early Church. He wrote several books in the New Testament. Some people believe he wrote 13 of them. There are only 27 books in the New Testament. This means... If we do the math... 13/27 equals... 48%. So, the Apostle Paul wrote almost 1/2 of our New Testament scriptures. WOW! That is amazing. Now, the Apostle Paul, in addition to writing a LOT, was a missionary. One of the places he went was a place called Galatia. This was a place found in Ancient Turkey. Paul had visited Galatia at least 2 times, and after one or both of this trips (we are not really sure) Paul decides to write them an epistle (religious letter). We call this letter the 9th book in the New Testament (Galatians). Paul tells the Galatians to "Walk in the Spirit." He also goes on to tell them in Galatians 5:22 there are "Fruits of the Spirit." How

Having Real Joy

Joy does not mean you will never have problems. Joy does not mean you will always have everything you want. Joy means you can look beyond your circumstances to see that Jesus loves you. Joy is thinking about how Jesus saved all of us from our sins and from having to be lost forever from God. Joy is helping others find Jesus so they can be saved. Joy is helping others so they have a good day. Joy is not allowing your attitude to grow bad because you do not want to do something you are asked to do.

Joy is not only for us to show God we love Him. Joy is not only for us to show others we are Christians. Joy helps us live good lives. When we are joyful, we are happier. When we are happier, our bodies respond to our happiness. We are not as sick. We feel better. Joy is a very important fruit to have.

I know there are times when all of us are sad. And God knows this too, but the best thing we can do is be sad only for a moment, and jump right back into being joyful to God. Try it this coming week. Let Jesus see your joy. Let others see your joy!

do we know if we are "walking in the Spirit"? We will be the "fruits of the Spirit."

The first of these fruits is LOVE! Christians should want to walk in the Spirit so we can be more like Jesus. So to do this, we should first LOVE others and LOVE Jesus.

Joy

In addition to LOVE, Paul instructs Christians who walk in the Spirit of God to have JOY! Other people always like to be around joyful people. There's something about having a good attitude that is infectious... or wants others to have it too. When you show joy at home, at school, at the store, or at church, you cause others to want to be joyful too. So, keep bringing the joy with you everywhere you go. This world needs a little joy!

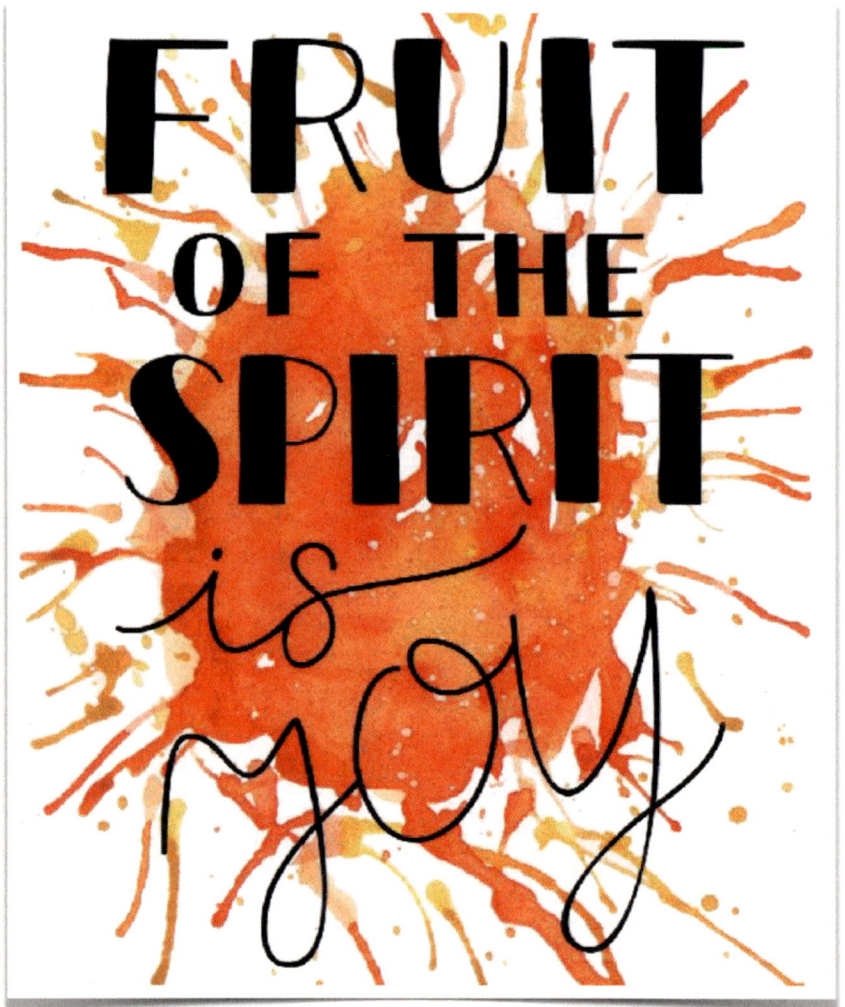

Why Do We Need the Fruits of the Spirit?

1. To bring hope to others.

2. To transform ourselves into better people of God.

3. To show that we are following Jesus' example He gave to all of us.

4. To please our Heavenly Father.

There are children all over the world who need Love & Joy in their lives. We can show those around us how much we love like Jesus. If you see someone who is not feeling well, help that person feel better. Talk to them. Show them you are a friend. Give them a snack. Play with them. You do not have to buy things to show the fruit of the Spirit. It all comes from within you. Be the fruit. Be Love. Be Joy. Think about all the Love that Jesus showed others while He was on this earth living as a human. Love like that. Think about all the Joy Jesus brought others while He was living on earth. Give Joy like that! It's not as hard as we think it is. Let's make sure our vines are full of LOVE & JOY!

Bearing Fruit

Write the Message Below:

MEMORY VERSE

Beloved, let us love one another: for love is of God; and every one that loveth is born of God, and knoweth God.

1 John 4:8

When we think about God, we realize that no man has ever really spent a lot of time watching God. Oh sure we can see the effects of His actions, but we don't really have the opportunity to watch what He does as He does it.

Jesus lived on Earth. For 33 1/2 years, men watched Jesus every day. Jesus was always trying to show His disciples and others how to live. Jesus showed love! Jesus showed joy!

Jesus said that we cannot even be Christians if we don't love each other. So, let's all work harder at taking on the Fruit of Love and Joy in our lives. We can do this. We can walk in the Spirit. We can please God with our lives. Jesus pleased the Father. Jesus loved the Father. We must do the same thing if we want to live in heaven forever with them.

DISCUSSION Q'S

1. A person in your class or home just spilled a tray of food all over the floor in the lunchroom or kitchen? What are some things you can do to show this person love? What are some things you can do to show this person joy?

2. You see a kid at the park who is playing by himself or herself on the see-saw. That person looks sad. What could you do to show this person love? What could you do to show this person joy?

3. What are some ways people can see your fruit? How do you show love? How do you show joy?

Knocking Down Barriers to Joy

Bowling for Joy:

Set up bowling set for kids.

Have each kid "bowl" for joy.

Keep score.

Have kids name the bowling pins after things that will steal their joy. Here are some examples:

- Bad grades

- Bad attitudes

- Fight with friends

- Fight with siblings

- Sickness, like a cold or COVID

- Family sick

Once kids are done playing the bowling game, continue to talk to them about how we can "knock out" things that steal our joy.

Verse:

Count it all joy, my brothers, when you meet trials of various kinds,

(James 1:2)

LET'S GIGGLE

As part of your outreach ministry to your elderly or adults in your church, have your students create a Giggle Card for someone. It can be a family member, friend, or elderly person in the Church.

Materials needed:

Blank Cards or Card stock paper, stickers, construction paper, glue sticks, markers, buttons, beads, feathers, or any other embellishment you may want to give them. Blank Envelopes for Cards. Help kids with messages to put in cards. You may want to print some out and let them paste them, or kids may be old enough to write their own messages. Make this fun. Make it at GIGGLE CARD!

Love & Joy

For each day of the week, look for a way to show love and joy to others around you. Put it in writing. Don't forget it!

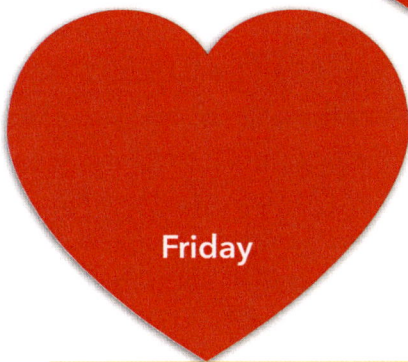

Monday

Tuesday

Wednesday

Thursday

Friday

Saturday

How did people respond to your Love and Joy this week? Make a journal note of what all happened.

PEACE & PATIENCE

Bearing Fruit for Jesus

Peace

Here are a few Bible Verses about PEACE:

Blessed are the peacemakers: for they shall be called the children of God.

I will both lay me down in peace, and sleep: for thou, Lord, only makest me dwell in safety.

Finally, brethren, farewell. Be perfect, be of good comfort, be of one mind, live in peace; and the God of love and peace shall be with you.

Longsuffering (Patience)

Here are a few Bible Verses about LONGSUFFERING (PATIENCE):

With all lowliness and meekness, with longsuffering, forbearing one another in love;

Put on therefore, as the elect of God, holy and beloved, bowels of mercies, kindness, humbleness of mind, meekness, longsuffering;

Peace

What does it mean to say you have the fruit of peace? Well, have you ever been in a situation where there was an argument? If you helped to find a solution, you were a peacemaker. God does not like conflict. Conflict comes from Satan, the devil. He is crafty and loves to start trouble. When we choose peace over war, we are bearing the fruit of peace. For example, if you have a group of friends who all want to go eat, and you love pizza, but the rest of the group loves burgers, you can be a peacemaker by choosing to have burgers too. Or if your mom and dad give you a set of chores to complete with your brother or sister, and you all argue about who will do which chore, that is not peace. But if you tell your brother or sister you will do which ever job, then that is making peace. It's not always easy to live in peace, but God honors us when we try. We are told in the Bible the peacemakers will be called the children of God. So, let's show peace to this world.

Longsuffering (Patience)

Do you have patience? Patience is hard. When you have to stand in line waiting for snacks, have you ever wanted to cut ahead? When you are at an amusement park, and the lines look like they go on forever, have you ever just wanted to skip ahead? It's hard to have patience for things in life. It's also hard to have patience with people. Taking turns on the playground, or waiting for a friend to get done with something so you can go to a movie - these things can try your patience. But the Bible tells us to have long-suffering, or patience, with others. So the next time you want to get in a rush, remember what the Apostle Paul said, "With all lowliness and meekness, with longsuffering, forbearing one another in love;" (Ephesians 4:2)

What does it take to have patience?

There are many ways we can show patience. Here is a list of 7:

1. Listening - when you listen to what others have to say, you are showing patience. Try to stop interrupting others when they are speaking.

2. Waiting - stop and think about waiting patiently in line the next time for snacks.

3. Quietness - sometimes when we want to tell people something that might hurt them, we hold our tongue.

4. No Rush - do not get in such a hurry to do everything. Sit and plan a while. Daydream; think about your future.

5. Others First - letting others go ahead is a cool thing to do.

6. Focus - do your tasks with focus. Don't rush through them.

7. Happy - be happy with what you have. Don't be so quick to do something else.

How Does Peace & Patience Help Others

1. **Peace and Patience with others helps us avoid unpleasant situations and tension.**

2. **Peace and Patience with others helps us to be part of a team who can get things done quickly and well.**

Think about how your interact with others. Are you a peacemaker or trouble maker? Be honest with yourself. If you always have to have things your way, you are likely not a peacemaker. If you are always upset with others, you likely do not have a lot of patience. Journal your feelings during the week and see which one you feel you are more like. If you are a peacemaker and patient person, keep doing what you are doing. If you find yourself unhappy and frustrated, work on become more peaceful and patient.

Peace & Patience

loud worry truce
calm
disagreement rough
fighting forgiving
quiet
upset gentle
unwilling
unity love friendship frustrated

Find the words associated with Peace & Patience and write them below:

Find the words opposite of Peace & Patience and write them below:

MEMORY VERSE

Blessed are the peacemakers: for they shall be called the children of God.

Matthew 5:9

Blessed - highly favored by God
Peacemaker - a person who brings about peace
Children - son or daughter of someone

When we make peace with others and for others we are blessed. We are the children of God. That means we enjoy all the privileges of being God's child. All His wealth is ours. All His power is for us. We are protected by Him, and we get to live in His Heaven when He is ready to call us to Him. Be a peacemaker. Live in the blessings of God. Be His child. It may seem hard at first, but the more you practice peace, the better you will become.

DISCUSSION Q'S

1. You have two friends at your home. One of the friends wants to watch a movie, and the other wants to play video games. You only have one TV and gaming console. What do you do to make peace?

2. You want to go to your friend's house, but your mother tells you that you have to clean your room first. You think for a moment that you want to be angry and pout, but what should you do to show patience and peace?

3. If a friend is having trouble with peace and patience, what are some things you can share with your friend to help them with peace and patience?

Going Bananas

Pass the Banana:

Materials needed:

Bananas

2 Teams

Graham crackers crushed or Vanilla wafers

Small plastic cups

Pudding prepared

Whipped topping

Have the kids in each team line up in a straight line, or you could try a large circle.

Have them sit down on the floor and place their feet forward.

Have the first kid pick up a banana with his/her feet.

Then have the kid pass the banana to the next person's feet. (If girls have on dresses, change the activity to the following:

Have kids get on knees.

Have the first kid roll the banana to the next person using only his/her chin.

The first team to pass the banana with feet (without dropping) or with chin wins.

Have prizes for winners, and others.

Use the bananas with pudding to make a cool treat.

Have pudding cups ready with graham cracker crust or vanilla wafers. Have pudding prepared in cups. Add sliced bananas on top for the kids who like them, and top off with whipped topping.

Love is patient, love is kind.
1 Corinthians 13:4

RECIPE FOR PATIENCE

As part of your outreach ministry to your elderly or adults in your church, have your students make "No Bake" Cookies. It can be a family

No Bake Cookies Recipe

Ingredients Needed:

1 ¾ cups white sugar

½ cup milk

½ cup butter

4 tablespoons unsweetened cocoa powder

½ cup crunchy peanut butter

3 cups quick-cooking oats

1 teaspoon vanilla extract

Directions:

In a medium saucepan, combine sugar, milk, butter, and cocoa. Bring to a boil, and cook for 1 1/2 minutes. Remove from heat, and stir in peanut butter, oats, and vanilla. Drop by teaspoonfuls onto wax paper. Let cool until hardened.

Makes 3 Dozen

Tasty no-bake cookies made with oatmeal, peanut butter and cocoa. Start timing when mixture reaches a full rolling boil; this is the trick to successful cookies. If you boil too long the cookies will be dry and crumbly. If you don't boil long enough, the cookies won't form properly.

Peace & Patience

For each day of the week, find someone you know who has shown peace or patience. Write down their actions. Tell how this helped you.

Monday

Tuesday

Wednesday

Thursday

Friday

Saturday

What did you learn from those around you who showed peace and patience this week? How will this help you have more patience and more peace in your own life?

KINDNESS & GOODNESS

Bearing Fruit for Jesus

KINDNESS

Here are a few Bible Verses about KINDNESS:

And be ye kind one to another, tenderhearted, forgiving one another, even as God for Christ's sake hath forgiven you.

She openeth her mouth with wisdom; and in her tongue is the law of kindness.

She openeth her mouth with wisdom; and in her tongue is the law of kindness.

GOODNESS

Here are a few Bible Verses about GOODNESS:

As we have therefore opportunity, let us do good unto all men, especially unto them who are of the household of faith.

But love ye your enemies, and do good, and lend, hoping for nothing again; and your reward shall be great, and ye shall be the children of the Highest: for he is kind unto the unthankful and to the evil.

KINDNESS

I love the quote, "In a world where you can be anything, be kind." I don't know who first said it, but it is a good quote. One thing I like to do is feed birds, and squirrels it seems. I think of this as an act of kindness. They do not do anything particular for me. I just love to watch them, but feeding something that cannot do anything in return for you, I think is kind. Holding the door open for people is an act of kindness. Giving a person food or a gift for no apparent reason is kindness. Allowing a friend to play with your games or toys is kindness. Smiling at a person who looks like he/she is having a bad day is kindness. Carrying the groceries for an elderly person is kindness. We could list 100s of kind acts. Kindness does not have to cost any money.

GOODNESS

Can We Be Good?

And Jesus said unto him, Why callest thou me good? there is none good but one, that is, God. (Mark 10:18)

Wait, what? Can no one really be good?   What did Jesus mean?

Well, since Adam and Eve sinned in the Garden, all mankind has been born with sin.   So we are "not" good. But, if we accept Jesus as our savior and pray to him to help us, then, YES, we can be good.   Jesus went on to say this, "One thing thou lackest: go thy way, sell whatsoever thou hast, and give to the poor, and thou shalt have treasure in heaven: and come, take up the cross, and follow me."

Jesus wanted the rich young ruler to realize that money does not make you good. Following Jesus makes you good. Let's all decide to follow Jesus.

King David wrote this in the 23rd Psalm: *Surely Goodness and Mercy shall follow me all the days of my life...*

He was talking about the "Goodness" of God following him. But the Apostle Paul was talking about our goodness when he wrote about the fruits of the Spirit. Goodness should still follow us from our own actions. We should always leave a room better than we found it. We should always try to have others see our goodness through Jesus.

We all have bad days. We all have days that we don't feel like being good, to be honest.   But because of God's goodness and the goodness of Christ, we should really work hard to be good.

Find a way to show the world your goodness fruit. There are many different ways. Pick one each day, and just be good. Come on! You can do it! Let Goodness follow you every single day of your life.

How can you be kind?

1. Put others first.

2. Listen to what others have to say.

3. Offer your help when you see others in need.

4. Carry a smile on your face and offer a helping hand.

5. Show compassion to those who hurt.

How can you be good?

1. Share a toy or game.

2. Hold the door open for someone.

3. Feed birds.

Kindness & Goodness

Random Acts of Kindness

```
Z W R D J C I Z B C L E A N I N G K F T
N R Y X O J C E O P X T S G Q O T D R K
G I V I N G A A Z O K O L E B H F C S S
U I W Q R N H W R C P Y M O W R R A E Y
L W X D N I X A D D A S F H W H C L L E
S Q Z R Y F H S H F U R O J P P O L Q X
I G D D Q B S H K O O M I P W Q N I J H
O B F E O K D I P L C F F N R X D N O F
F V L E G K E N D D H E A Z G E V G S S
U A O Z L L T G X I O V Z M G I S M D T
Z G W E L E O C T N C G D T K E X E F N
W J E I O X G L A G O I J F E J O S N X
A J R D V Y Z O T O L F A F O X F P Q T
W L S T E P S T I T A T L E V O T L S B
W A Q A G T M H Y R T S Z D B M D I X Q
Y U K L Y I R E I G E K Q W I M W V N P
R F X K U T Q S T C Q J S L X S W I R G
Z I V I L V D Y T X N J M F C W H F U I
H W E N X Y L Q Q T U A M K M T C E P K
Q T S G L Z L S V B U Y H U G S R E S M
```

chocolate	cleaning	washing	gifts
folding	texting	calling	hugs
present	talking	flowers	toys
clothes	giving	caring	card
dishes	love	food	buy

Kindness & Goodness

Why do you think the Apostle Paul put "forgiving" one another in with kindness? Isn't it wonderful to know that God will "forgive" us our sins? He is a Good, Good Father. He is Kind! He is tenderhearted. If we are to be like Christ or God, we must be kind. We must be good. Even when people do not deserve it.   God forgave us as sinners even though we were not good.   He loved us so much that He was willing to give all for our forgiveness.   We should do the same. Let's be kind! Let's be good!

MEMORY VERSE

And be ye kind one to another, tenderhearted, forgiving one another, even as God for Christ's sake hath forgiven you.

Ephesians 4:32

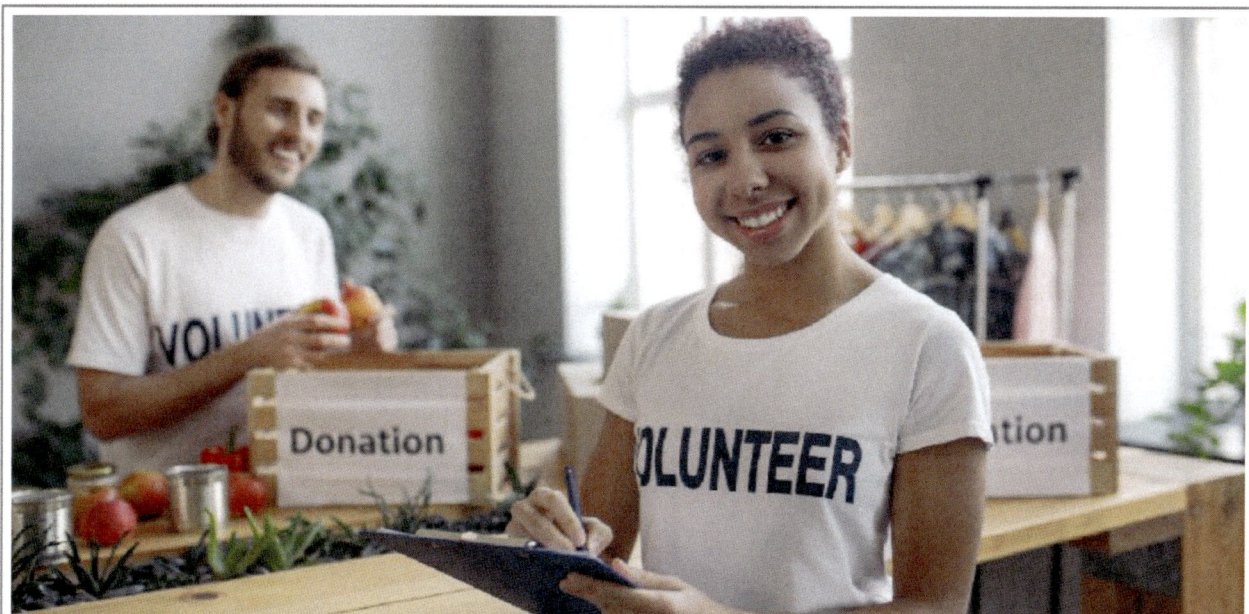

DISCUSSION Q'S

1. How are "Kindness" and "Goodness" alike? How are these two fruit different?

2. When we talk about the "goodness" of God? What do we mean? How does God show that he is "Good"?

3. List some ways you can be kind or good to a family member. List some ways you can be kind or good to a friend. List some ways you can be kind or good to animals. Think about how God has shown his goodness to these same people.

Making You Smile

I Can Make You Smile!

Materials needed:

Tennis Ball

Permanent Marker

Upbeat Music

Step 1: Make a smiley face on the Tennis Ball before Class.

Step 2: Put kids in a circle.

Step 3: Start playing upbeat music as kids toss the tennis ball from one kid to another. The objective is first to not have the tennis ball when the music stops.

Step 4: Once the music stops, the person who has the tennis ball must make those around him/her in the circle smile or laugh. The person gets a point for each person in the circle who smiles or laughs. The music starts again. The ball is tossed again until the music stops. And the game continues.

Surely goodness and mercy shall follow me all the days of my life: and I will dwell in the house of the LORD for ever.

Psalm 23:6

DO GOOD JAR

This activity is for each kid to create a "Do Good" Jar of activities. Then the kids will take them home and each week pull a Popsicle stick out to see what they can do for others. Have fun making the jars with your students and the Popsicle "Do Good" Messages. Experiment. We will give you a few ideas, but have your students think of more. It would be great if each jar could be filled with ideas for the kids.

Materials Needed:

Jars

Sticky Labels

Popsicle Sticks

Sharpie Markers

Color Markers for Labels

Directions:

1. Make a label for your jar. You may want to call it the "Do Good Jar" or "Random Acts of Kindness" or whatever you decide. Just label it your jar.

2. Color your labels

3. Color your popsicle sticks.

4. Write a "Do Good" or "Random Act of Kindness" on each popsicle stick. See if you can do at least 20.

5. Take home, and try to do at least 1 random act of kindness or do-good activity each week. Tell your class about your activities.

My Do Good Jar

Wash the dishes
Fold the clothes
Take out the garbage
Make something for someone
Volunteer to clean someone's yard
Send someone a card
Share a snack with someone
Clear the table
Clean out the car
Visit someone who is lonely
Read someone a story

Kindness & Goodness

For each day of the week, plan an act of kindness and an act of goodness. Record what you do each day. Tell how this made you feel.

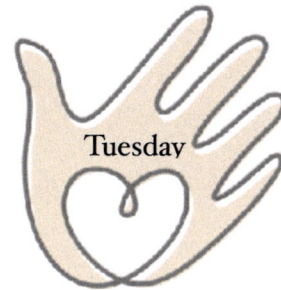

Monday -

_____

_____

Tuesday -

_____

_____

Wednesday -

_____

_____

Thursday -

_____

_____

Friday -

_____

_____

Saturday -

_____

_____

Did you find others who were perhaps kind or good to you? Talk about what you experienced and how it made you feel.

FAITH & MEEKNESS

Bearing Fruit for Jesus

FAITH

Here are a few Bible Verses about FAITH:

For we walk by faith, not by sight.

And Jesus said unto him, Go thy way; thy faith hath made thee whole.

Now faith is the substance of things hoped for, the evidence of things not seen.

But without faith it is impossible to please him:

MEEKNESS

Here are a few Bible Verses about MEEKNESS:

Blessed are the meek: for they shall inherit the earth.

Take my yoke upon you, and learn of me; for I am meek and lowly in heart: and ye shall find rest unto your souls.

With all lowliness and meekness, with longsuffering, forbearing one another in love;

FAITH

It is not always easy to have faith. During a storm, when the winds are blowing, and you feel like the world will come crashing down around you, having faith can be a little difficult. But God wants us to believe in Him. We have to trust His process. We have to trust that He is working all things for our good, and not evil. The devil wants us to doubt God. He placed the first doubt in Eve's mind in the Garden of Eden. He told her God was keeping things from her so she would not be like God. God had a perfect plan for mankind, and the devil did not like it. So he made sure Adam and Eve sinned against God. Jesus tells us over and over that we must have faith. He healed people because they had faith in God. He performed miracles because of their faith. Learn to trust the process. Learn to trust God.

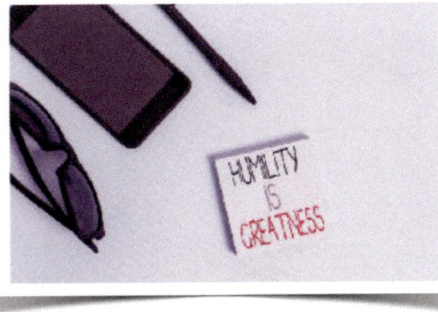

Humility is Hard!

Being humble in all situations is hard. We love ourselves. We want to go first. We want to take care of our own selves. But what does Jesus have to say about being humble?

In Matthew 23:12, Jesus says this. If you humble yourself, God will lift you up. But if you lift yourself up, God will cause you to fall low.

Jesus also told a story in Luke 18. There were two men who came into the temple (kind of like our church) to pray. One man, a Pharisee, boasted to God of how he had given in the offering and all the good things he had done and times he fasted. The other man, a tax collector, prayed to God to help him for he had sinned. Jesus said the tax collector went away justified (forgiven) before God. The Pharisee went away with all his pride that would surely make him fall and disappointment from God. Be humble.

MEEKNESS

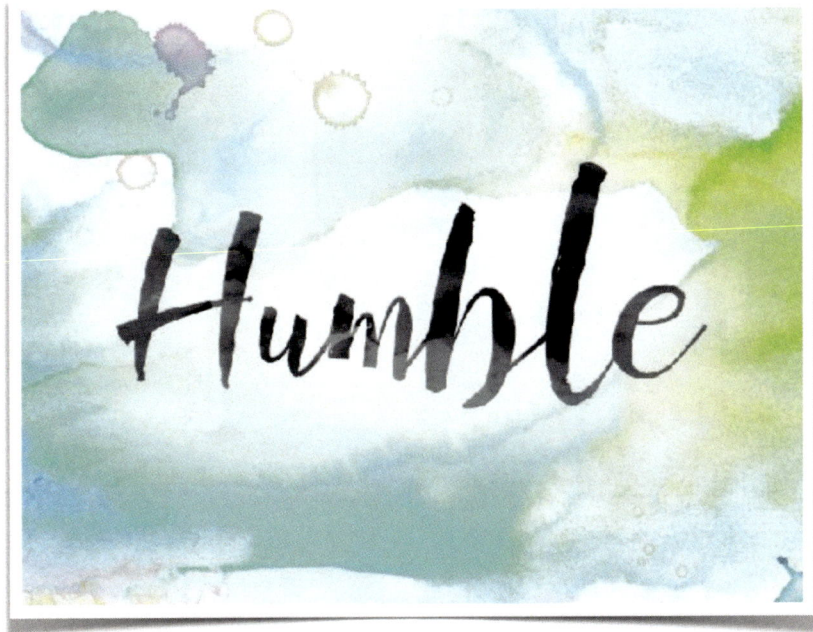

What does it mean to be meek? Let's look at the definition of "meekness." Merriam-Webster says meekness is "a mild, moderate, humble, or submissive quality". Let's put it this way. If your mom tells you to clean your room, and you say, "I don't want to clean my room," is this meekness? Not exactly. But if your mom tells you to clean your room, and you say, "Sure, Mom, I'm happy to do it," that displays meekness. If you have friends playing kickball or football, and you don't get picked on the team you like best, what should you do to show meekness? That's right, be on the other team and play with all your might without complaining. Meekness means you do not always have to have your way or be first. Meekness means you prefer other people to go first or have the best spots. Now let's face it: It's not easy to be meek. But God sees this as a great quality. God says, "If you can be humble here, I'll give you everything you desire later." For in the Bible God tells is that "The meek shall inherit the earth." So the next time someone wants to push ahead of you, let them. Keep the main goal in mind.

Ways to Strengthen Faith

1. Pray every day.

2. Read the word of God.

3. Study faithful people in the Bible.

4. Keep a record of prayers God answers.

5. Surround yourself with people of faith.

6. Believe that God is always trustworthy.

Show Meekness!

1. Give credit to others when they do good things.

2. Be patient with others.

3. Allow others to go first.

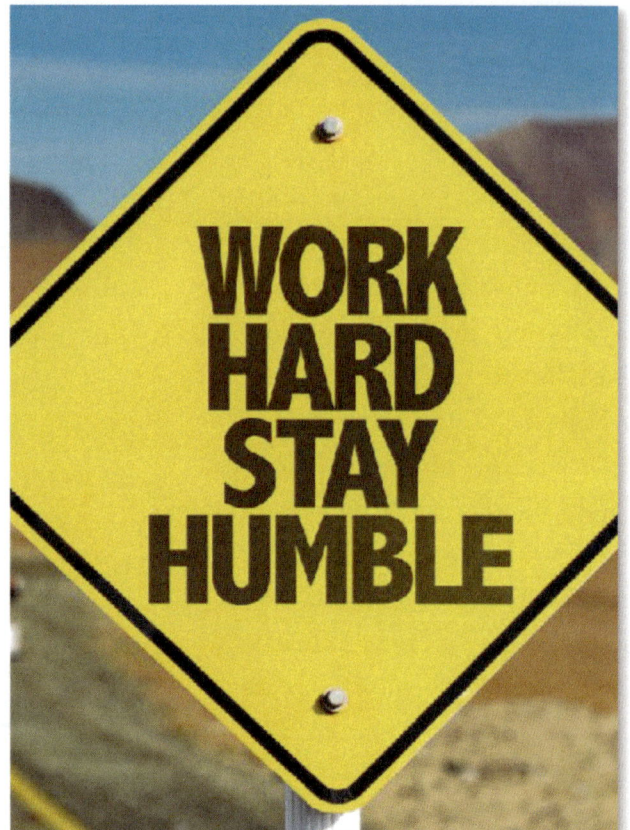

WORK HARD STAY HUMBLE

Faith & Meekness

```
T  S  A  K  E  M  Y  Y  O  K  E  U  P  O  N
Y  S  O  U  A  N  D  L  E  A  R  N  O  F  M
E  E  F  O  R  I  A  M  M  E  E  K  A  N  D
L  N  O  W  L  Y  I  N  H  E  A  R  T  A
N  K  D  A  L  L  T  H  I  N  G  T  S  W  H
A  E  T  S  O  E  V  E  R  Y  E  I  S  H  A
L  E  L  A  S  K  I  N  P  R  A  A  Y  E  R
B  M  E  L  I  E  V  I  N  G  Y  F  E  S  H
A  L  L  R  E  C  E  I  V  E  Y  S  P  F  D
Z  C  B  V  T  N  A  J  A  J  F  H  Y  P  D
W  L  Z  I  K  P  O  E  S  G  U  L  X  G  V
N  L  V  X  O  Q  W  K  H  X  C  U  P  M  M
Q  C  R  S  T  P  C  Q  D  T  A  Y  A  M  T
E  P  L  N  M  C  S  X  E  K  L  F  Y  I  U
Y  P  J  H  G  J  D  C  H  I  J  E  J  T  X
```

Faith   Meekness

__ ___ __ _____ ____

___, ____ _____ ___

__; ____ _ __ ___

___ _____ __

_____: ____ ___

_____, _____

__ _____ ___ __

____, _____

__ _____ _____.

What did Jesus say about "Faith" and "Meekness?"

Here are two scriptures the Lord told us about faith and meekness. But before you find them, you must find the words "Faith" and "Meekness" Cross out those two clues, and then the rest of the message should be easy. Put each word of the message in the blanks provide. Happy Scripture Hunting!

Based on these scriptures of Jesus' words, what do you think Jesus feels about your faith and your meekness?

Faith

Jesus tells his disciples that their faith can move mountains. He tells them to have faith in God, and not to doubt. We have to have faith in order to please God. We have to believe God is working all things for our good. Even when we are sick... Even when things do not happen like we plan... Even if we fail at something... We have to believe God loves us and is working things out for us. Never lose your faith in God. He is the only one we need in this life to perform all things in our favor and for our good. It's okay to believe in others, but know they may let you down. However, know that God never fails you. Jesus is always praying for you. Build your faith in them. Stand strong in your faith in God.

MEMORY VERSE

Therefore I say unto you, What things soever ye desire, when ye pray, believe that ye receive them, and ye shall have them.

Mark 11:24

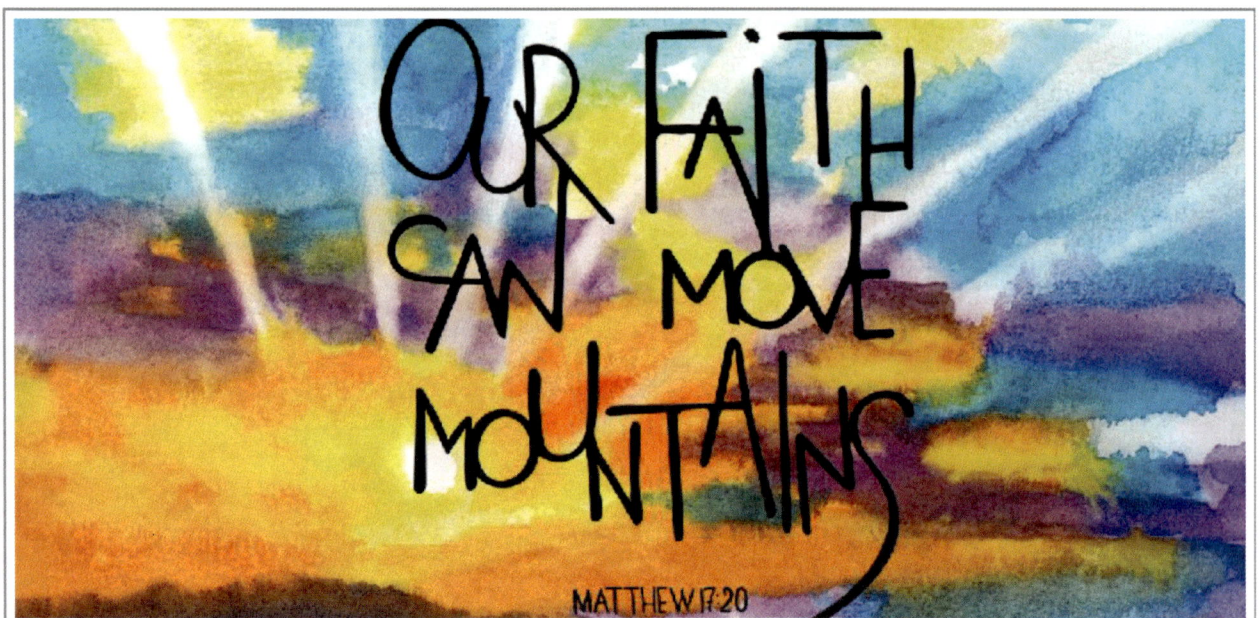

DISCUSSION Q'S

1. How large is your faith in God? What are somethings that could cause doubt?

2. How meek or humble are you? What are some difficult areas in your life for you to show humility?

3. We are told to have faith in God, but faith is not always easy. We need to grow our faith. What are some ways in which we can continue to grow our faith each day?

Live Humbly

Show Your Humility

Materials needed:

Basketball or Kickball or Beachball

Timer

Step 1: Place kids in a line in two teams if you have enough kids. One team is fine if you do not.

Step 2: Tell them to practice passing (throwing gently) the ball to each other while saying their ABCs.

Step 3: Now tell them the real game begins.

Step 4: Each person must throw the ball backwards to the next person while saying the next letter in the alphabet BACKWARDS each time.

Z Y X W V U T S R Q P O N M L K J I H G F E D C B A

If a person drops the ball or misses the letter, the ball has to go back to the front and the kids must start the alphabet backwards all over again. The team to finish all of the alphabet first wins. If there are only enough kids for one team, then just have them try for 5 minutes and see how far they got. Let them try again and see if they get better.

Who is a wise man and endued with knowledge among you? let him shew out of a good conversation his works with meekness of wisdom.

James 3:13

TELLING MY STORY

This is an opportunity for kids to tell their story as a testimony for others. Their stories can be placed on the church social media page.

Materials Needed:

Video Camera

Parental Consent for posting

Directions:

1. **Video Version** - Have kids tell their story of faith and post it on the Lighthouse of Living Faith Social Media page. (Or on your own church's Social Media page)

   OR

2. **Picture/Testimony Version** - Post a picture of the child's testimony after he/she has written it on paper.

> Telling others your testimony of your faith in Jesus is another way to build your faith. Here's a template to use for the video or testimony version:
>
> My name is _____.
>
> I attend _____ church.
>
> I believe in God because _____
> _____.
>
> I am trying to build my faith by _____
> _____.
>
> I hope my testimony is a blessing to you.

Faith & Meekness

For each day of the week, think of a way you can build your faith or show humility to others.

Monday

Tuesday

Monday -
_____
_____

Tuesday -
_____
_____

Wednesday

Thursday

Wednesday -
_____
_____

Thursday -
_____
_____

Friday

Saturday

Friday -
_____
_____

Saturday -
_____
_____

At the end of the week, talk about how your faith has grown. What helped you? What tried your faith?

TEMPERANCE (SELF-CONTROL)

Bearing Fruit for Jesus

TEMPERANCE

Here are a few Bible Verses about TEMPERANCE:

And as he reasoned of righteousness, temperance, and judgment to come, Felix trembled, and answered, Go thy way for this time; when I have a convenient season, I will call for thee.

Meekness, temperance: against such there is no law.

And to knowledge temperance; and to temperance patience; and to patience godliness;

And every man that striveth for the mastery is temperate in all things. Now they do it to obtain a corruptible crown; but we an incorruptible.

He that is slow to anger is better than the mighty; and he that ruleth his spirit than he that taketh a city.

He that hath no rule over his own spirit is like a city that is broken down, and without walls.

SELF-CONTROL

Have you ever just wanted to scream, but you knew you probably shouldn't? What did you do? Did you scream? Did it help? Or did you use self-control and just keep on doing what you needed to do? Having temperance (or self control) is not easy. Or maybe it is easier for some than it is for others. But when things go wrong in our lives, we tend to want to let out our frustration. But self control is not just about holding back our feelings. It is also about holding back our desires. If we eat until we are sick, we are not using self-control. If we play video games all night long and get no sleep, we are not using self-control. If we spend more money than we actually have or need to spend, we are not using self-control. Self control is about all areas of our lives. We need to control what we do in all things.

REVIEW of FRUITS

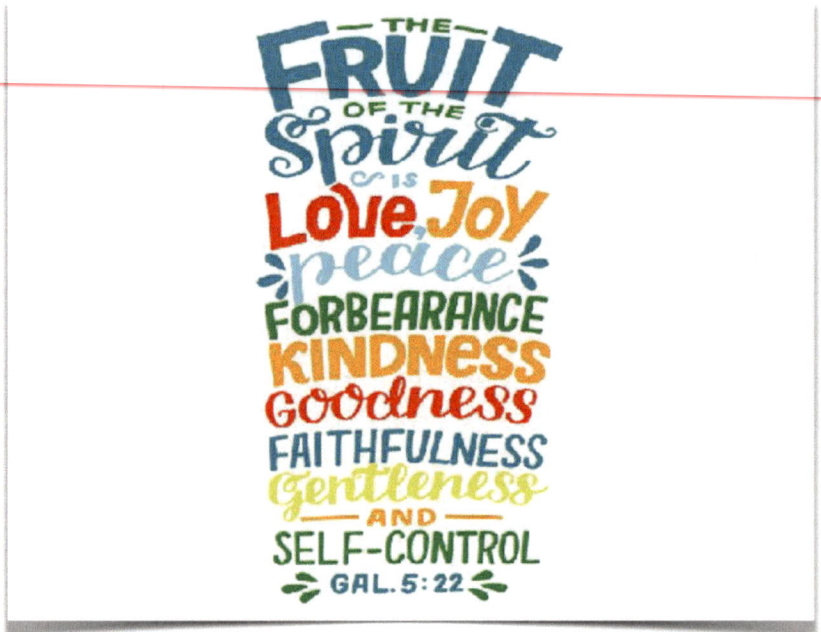

Bearing Fruit!

This unit of lessons has been about becoming better examples of Christians through bearing fruit for God. It is not always easy to bear good fruit. What causes us to stop?

1. Just things that happen in life. Sometimes we are sick. Sometimes we are angry. Sometimes we feel alone. It's okay to have these feelings for a moment, but then we have to remember who loves us. God loves us. We have to rise above problems.

2. Our pride and our desire to have it all. Sometimes our biggest problem is in the mirror. We hurt ourselves by wishing for things that God does not want us to have or things we do not need. So, we just have to say "NO" to us.

Over the past few weeks, we have studied all nine fruits of the Spirit: Love, Joy, Peace, Patience, Kindness, Goodness, Faith, Meekness, and Temperance. These are all listed in Galatians 5:22. When we show these fruit in our lives, we show we are being led by the Spirit of God. What have we learned from our study? Let's recap:

1. We should show LOVE to all mankind, especially our family, friends, and neighbors.
2. We should be JOYful in our daily lives, not grumpy and mean.
3. We should have PEACE in our hearts and live at peace with others.
4. We should be PATIENT towards others and ourselves.
5. We should show KINDNESS to all living things, especially people around us.
6. We should have GOODNESS in our hearts to do the right things.
7. We should be full of FAITH in God and be faithful to God.
8. We should have a GENTLE or meek spirit.
9. We should have SELF CONTROL in all areas of our life.

How to have Self-Control

1. Get away from things that tempt you to do wrong.

2. Set goals for yourself to monitor what you do.

3. Exercise, sing, play music or games, walk, do things to keep you under control.

4. Stay focused on what is important for you to be successful and happy.

5. Learn from mistakes; forgive yourself; move forward.

Examples of Losing Self-Control!

1. Fight with those around you.

2. Throwing things.

3. Yelling or screaming.

4. Eating so much you get sick.

5. Taking what does not belong to you.

6. Doing things you know are wrong.

7. Trying to hide things you do from parents or teacher.

Self-Control

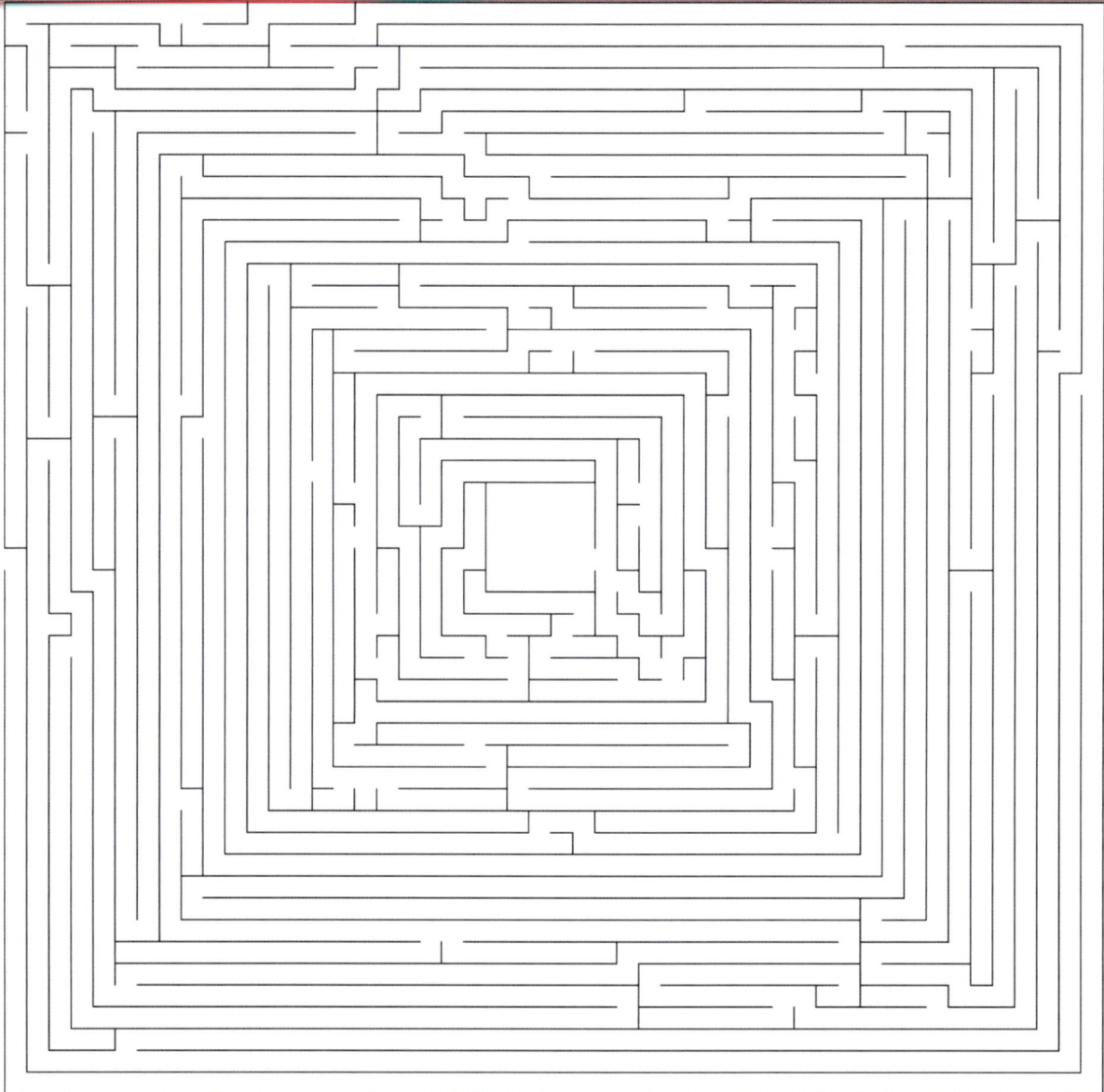

How well did you complete this maze?

Did you get tired of it?

Did you get frustrated?

What did this maze teach you about your own self-control?

Fruit of the Spirit

If there is one thing I like most about all fruit it is that fruit is SWEET! It tastes good. Well, most fruit is sweet. But when you think about a grape, apple, banana, or blueberry, you think that you are going to have something sweet. Our lives should be pleasing for others to be around us. Our fruit is important. We need to make sure we are bearing good fruit. So, go forth, bear your fruit to the world. Make sure it is sweet!

MEMORY VERSE

But the fruit of the Spirit is love, joy, peace, longsuffering, gentleness, goodness, faith, Meekness, temperance: against such there is no law.

Galatians 5:22-23

DISCUSSION Q'S

1. What are some areas of your life where you struggle with self-control?

2. How can you challenge yourself to gain more self-control each day?

3. Of all the nine fruits of the SPIRIT, which ones did you find easier to have in your life? Which ones did you find harder to have in your life?

Clap Like Me

Show Your Self-Control

Materials needed:

Students

Teacher

Step 1: Have students sitting in a row or around a table.

Step 2: Start the students with a simple clap pattern using your hands only. Like this: Clap, Hold, Clap, Clap, Hold, Clap, Clap, Clap.)

Step 3: Students have to all replicate the same clap pattern just like you.

Step 4: Now let the next student create his/her own clap pattern. Everyone has to replicate it. If anyone messes up, you have to go back to the beginning (you) and start over.

Alternative Version: Handmade Drums Required

You could also make drums and use your hands on the drums for the drum pattern.

Alternative Version: DIY Maracas

You can also make DIY maracas and use them for a shake pattern.

PUTTING A LITTLE FRUIT IN YOUR WATER

This is an opportunity for kids to share the Gospel while decorating water bottles with a message. Use the Fruits of the Spirit for kids to think of messages: Love, Joy, Peace, Faith, Goodness, Patience, Kindness, Meekness, Self-Control

Materials Needed:

Water Bottles Unopened.

Flavored Water Packets

Cards, paper, tape, or labels

Directions:

1. **Have students create a message for their water bottle.**

2. **Place message on water bottle.**

3. **Tape a fruit flavored water pack to bottle.**

4. **Have students take water bottles and pass out in church, and take some home to pass out to mail person, coach, bus driver, or others. (Parental permission needed).**

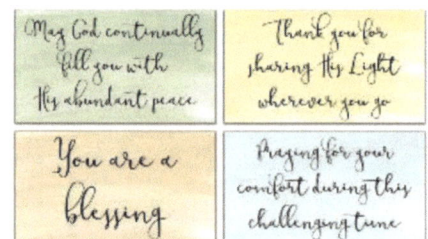

Self-Control

For each day of the week, think of a way you can show self-control.

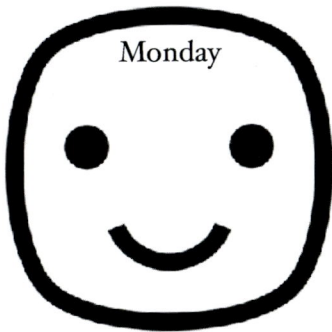

Monday

Tuesday

Wednesday

Monday -

_____

_____

Tuesday -

_____

_____

Wednesday -

_____

_____

Thursday -

_____

_____

Friday -

_____

_____

Saturday -

_____

_____

Thursday

Friday

Saturday

How well did you control things in your life this week? What did you improve? Where did you still need more help?

Made in the USA
Coppell, TX
13 April 2024

31255909R00031